"To date, resources specifically for traumatized teens have not been readily available, despite the fact that many experience traumatic events during childhood and into their teen years. This book, *The PTSD Workbook for Teens*, offers much-needed information aimed at the special needs of this population. Author Libbi Palmer addresses the main after-effects of trauma and offers practical information and worksheets to help teen readers work through their symptoms and reestablish safety, personal control, and positive self-esteem. I highly recommend it."

—Christine A. Courtois, PhD, ABPP, psychologist and author of *Treating Complex Traumatic Stress Disorder*, and *The Treatment of Complex Trauma*

"Palmer has provided teens with a terrific resource to understand, process, and heal from trauma. The book is quite comprehensive but easy to use, and gives teens the power to choose at what level they want to work through their issues. These are techniques that really work to help teens move on from bad experiences and feel better."

—Carrie Merscham, PsyD, psychologist and author of the blog selfhelponthego.com

"Palmer has a powerful grasp on the needs of teenagers and a user-friendly approach to trauma recovery. This workbook provides hands-on tools, easily accessible by a teen working through trauma alone, or for treatment providers looking for a framework to help adolescent clients overcome trauma. Work through this book and find a road to peace."

—Ambra Born, PsyD, Director of child psychological services at Reaching HOPE in Lakewood, CO

the
ptsd workbook
for teens

simple, effective skills
for **healing trauma**

LIBBI PALMER, PsyD

Instant Help Books
A Division of New Harbinger Publications, Inc.

Distributed in Canada by Raincoast Books

Copyright © 2012 by Libbi Palmer
        Instant Help Books
        A Division of New Harbinger Publications, Inc.
        5674 Shattuck Avenue
        Oakland, CA 94609
        www.newharbinger.com

Cover design by Amy Shoup

Library of Congress Cataloging-in-Publication Data

Palmer, Libbi.
 The PTSD workbook for teens : simple, effective skills for healing trauma / Libbi Palmer.
   p. cm.
 ISBN 978-1-60882-321-5 (pbk. : alk. paper) -- ISBN 978-1-60882-322-2 (pdf e-book) -- ISBN 978-1-60882-323-9 (epub)
 1. Post-traumatic stress disorder in adolescence--Treatment. 2. Cognitive therapy for teenagers. I. Title.
 RJ506.P55P35 2012
 616.85'2100835--dc23

              2012019239

Printed in the United States of America

14   13   12

10   9   8   7   6   5   4   3   2   1

First Printing

To G. B. P., with love and gratitude for your unwavering support.

contents

✳ contents

Dear Reader,

Welcome to *The PTSD Workbook for Teens: Simple, Effective Skills for Healing Trauma.* You may have picked up this book for a lot of different reasons. Maybe you recently experienced a traumatic event, or maybe it was something that happened a long time ago. More than one traumatic event may have happened to you. You may not even be sure that what happened to you was trauma. Maybe you are close to someone who has faced a trauma, and you want to know more about it. Someone may have suggested that this book would be helpful. Maybe more than one of these scenarios fits your situation. Whatever the case, this book is for you.

This book will help you understand what trauma is and how it often affects people. You will also learn skills that will help you manage the effects of the trauma. The initial activities in the book are aimed at helping you tell the story of your trauma in a way that makes it not hurt so much. The later activities in the book are focused on helping you move forward with the rest of your life now that you have addressed your trauma.

It may seem strange to you that in a book about healing from trauma, you aren't asked to talk in detail about your trauma until almost the end of the book. This is not by accident. It's important that you have the knowledge and skills in place to manage your reactions and to keep yourself safe before trying to process the trauma. So, skills come first. By the time you have the necessary skills, writing about the trauma in detail will be a relatively easy part of the healing process.

Each activity in this book will offer information for you to learn and at least one action for you to take. Some of the activities will be more important to you than others, but they build on each other, so it's best to go through the activities in order, at least the first time. You may find that you need to practice the skills from some activities more than others to get really good at them, and you may need to go back and review some activities later.

You may feel an urge to rush through this book just to "get it over with." That urge is completely understandable. Who wouldn't want to just be done with a trauma? I would like to encourage you to work through this book in a systematic way. Healing happens naturally if you are given enough time and support from the people around you. This book is designed to help you understand what's happening to you, to keep you relatively safe during the healing process, and to speed that process along as much as possible. Although the book will work with the natural healing that will take place anyway, if you rush through it too quickly, the effects of the trauma may not completely heal. Please take your time and work through each activity as thoroughly as you can. It will be best in the long run if you do.

You may decide to work through this book alone. The activities are designed to let you do that. Some people seek help from a professional, like a counselor, therapist, psychologist, social worker, or psychiatrist. This book may be something that you work on and share with that person. You may also decide to share the work you do in this book, or parts of it, with other people. Whom you share it with is completely up to you.

The overall concept for this book is based on the work of Dr. Judith L. Herman, a renowned psychiatrist, and *trauma-focused cognitive behavioral therapy*, which was developed by Dr. Judith A. Cohen, an innovative psychiatrist, and esteemed psychologists Anthony P. Mannarino and Esther Deblinger. The skills this book teaches are primarily from cognitive therapy, which was developed by Dr. Aaron Beck. It's not important for you to remember those names, but you can be confident that this book is based on work that is well known to help people heal from the traumatic experiences they have faced.

Congratulations for taking this first step in healing from your trauma.

a letter to parents

Dear Parents,

If you have picked up this book, your teen has probably experienced some kind of traumatic event. This book is designed for teens who have undergone a variety of traumas: natural disasters, assaults, abuse, deaths of loved ones, or any other event in the teen's life that seemed traumatic.

You may be wondering about the best way for you to support your teen. There are a few things that are important for you to know to help your teen through the healing process:

- When someone you love experiences a traumatic event, it's traumatizing for you too. Be sure to take care of yourself and get the support you need to help yourself through this difficult time. If you don't take care of yourself, you won't be able to help your teen.

- Trauma affects people in physical, emotional, and behavioral ways. You may notice changes in any or all of these areas in your teen. This is to be expected. This book can help your teen address each of these areas.

- Most people heal from most traumatic events with mere time and the support of the people who care about them. You and your teen may decide that additional support from a mental health professional is necessary. Assistance like this can help your teen learn skills to manage reactions to the trauma and heal faster. Professional help is especially important if your teen is engaging in risky behaviors like drug or alcohol use, or self-harm.

- Teens need as much normalcy as possible while they are trying to heal. This means that your teen should be allowed to do the same things as before, even if it makes you anxious to let her out of your sight. It also means that she needs the limits that you have always placed on her, so it's important that you continue to set and enforce rules for your teen.

- Support from people close to us helps us heal from trauma. It's important that you support your teen, but because teens normally have their closest relationships with friends, it's also important for your teen to spend time with his friends and others who support him.

- Teens need some privacy. It's important for your teen to share with you how she is doing and how you can support her. It may also be important that she have some privacy, so let her share with you as she chooses from this book, from her therapy, and from her experiences overall.

I want to reemphasize that most people heal from trauma without long-lasting effects. Your support and the tools in this book will make it even more likely that your teen will heal from his experiences.

sharing this book, or not

for you to know

Healing from trauma is a very personal process. You can choose how you use this book. One way of getting some feelings of safety back into your life is to decide where you will keep this book and with whom you will share it.

Because you may write some very personal details in this book, you may decide to keep it where no one will see it without your permission. You may choose to share parts of this book and some of the things you write. It's important that you get to choose what you share and when you share it. Maybe you are seeing a mental health professional, like a counselor, psychologist, or social worker. You might use this book in that work or decide to share it with that person.

Some of the traumas people experience are from nature, like earthquakes and tornadoes, but some traumas are caused by other people. Sometimes the person who has been traumatized wants to confront the person who caused the distress. If this is your situation, you may decide to share this book or parts of it later, but I recommend that you at least wait until you have finished working through the book. Then you can decide what you share.

Michael buys this book to help himself heal from being emotionally abused by his mother. He decides to keep the book in a locked drawer in his desk so that no one will be able to read it without his permission.

Jessica has been seeing a counselor since she was traumatized, and the counselor suggested that she buy this book. They are going to work on the exercises in the book together during their sessions.

Chris has been talking with his parents and his best friend about the trauma that he experienced, and he plans to share some of the activities from this book with them. Chris is going to keep the book on the top of his bookshelf to make sure that his younger siblings don't read it. He may decide to share parts of it with them when they are older, but until then, he wants to make sure they don't read it.

for you to do

Answer the following questions about your particular situation:

Where are you going to keep this book to make sure it gets shared only with the people you want to share it with?

_____

_____

_____

_____

_____

Whom do you know that you want to share this book or parts of it with?

_____

_____

_____

Whom are you sure, at least for now, that you do not want to share this book with?

_____

_____

_____

---

for you to know

Trauma is an event that usually involves death or serious injury, or the threat of death or serious injury. The actual event doesn't have to happen to you directly; it can happen to someone close to you. Trauma is an event that is so frightening or painful that it overwhelms you and interferes with the ways that you usually cope with difficult events in your life. The event might have arisen from a natural disaster, like a hurricane, a tornado, or an earthquake. Or it might be something caused by things someone did, whether on purpose, like assault or abuse, or accidentally, like a car crash.

Everyone experiences events in different ways. How you respond during and after a trauma depends on many factors, including:

- How close you were to the event

- What the event was

- How much support you got from the people around you

- What else was happening in your life at the time

- What else happened in your life in the past

You may have picked up this book or been given the book in response to a particular event, but there may have been other traumatic events in your life. It's important to recognize all of the possible events in your life that might have been traumatic, even if you are sure you are over them. You can decide later if you need to do any further activities around the traumas that you think you have healed from.

Matt was recently bitten by a neighbor's dog and seriously injured. He had to have surgery and will always have some scars from the attack. His current reactions remind him of when he was frightened, confused, and angry after being chased by a dog as a young child.

Ashley is shocked and overwhelmed when she learns that her sister has been in a plane crash during her vacation. Even though Ashley is perfectly safe, she has trouble catching her breath, concentrating, and controlling her emotions.

for you to do

The following is a list of possible traumas. It's not a complete list, so there are lines at the end for you to add other events. Write an "X" in the first column for traumas that you have experienced. Then, for each event you have experienced, write an "X" in the column after that kind of trauma to tell whether you think it might still be affecting you.

I have experienced this kind of event.	Traumatic Event	This still affects me.	This does not still affect me.	I'm not sure if this still affects me.
	Dog bite			
	Car accident			
	Child abuse (physical)			
	Sexual abuse			
	Sexual assault			
	Physical assault			
	Significant injury			
	Robbery			
	Serious illness			
	Being threatened			
	Sudden death of a loved one			
	Domestic violence			
	Parents' divorce			
	Death of a pet			
	Natural disaster (tornado, earthquake, hurricane, and so on)			
	Other:			
	Other:			
	Other:			

...and more to do

Now look at the traumatic events that you marked in the previous chart.

What were things like right after those events happened?

_____

_____

_____

_____

_____

What was it like after some time passed (a few months or more)?

_____

_____

_____

_____

What was helpful to you after those events?

_____

_____

_____

_____

_____

What was not helpful to you after those events?

_____

_____

_____

_____

_____

healing from trauma

---

for you to know

Unfortunately, trauma is something that many people experience during their lives. Many people heal from trauma with time and with their loved ones supporting them. Healing is a natural process that most people go through, but sometimes, extra help is needed to make the healing easier and this book may be that extra help you need. You may have experienced a trauma in the past that you have healed from, and you may have learned things from that healing that will help you heal from your current trauma.

One of the reasons it's important to heal from trauma is that you might experience trauma again in your life. If you heal from a trauma and then experience another trauma, you will have an easier time healing from the second trauma than you would if you had never experienced trauma before or had experienced a trauma before but not healed from it. You can look at this like getting a vaccination from your medical doctor. The doctor gives you a small dose of a virus in order to protect you from the virus in the future.

Sometimes people need help knowing how to heal. You will learn in upcoming chapters that one common response to trauma is to avoid reminders of the events, and another is to think about the trauma all the time, even when you don't want to. Without some guidance in knowing how to heal from trauma, some people think they should just keep talking about it and they will heal, while others think that if they just move on and try not to think or talk about it, everything will be fine. As you may have guessed, neither of these extreme ways of dealing with trauma is the best way to heal.

This book can help you find ways to heal from trauma, but healing takes time and effort on your part. You will need to learn and practice skills that will help you heal. It's important that you make a commitment to healing from the trauma you experienced. One of the activities ahead will help you weigh the pros and cons of going through the healing process right now. If you decide that this is not the right time, this book and other ways of healing will be available to you when you decide it's the right time.

Emily was sexually assaulted at a party. She commits to healing from her trauma and working through this book in order to get her life back to normal.

Josh was abused by his father when he visited him during a vacation. He has to go back to see his father in the next few weeks, so he plans to wait until after he returns home before doing anything more than learning the skills at the beginning of this book. He thinks these skills will help him, but he needs to wait until he is back at his mother's house before he processes the actual abusive events.

Sarah was in a bad car accident when she was in elementary school. She is using some of the things she remembers about healing from that accident to help her with her current trauma. For example, she remembers that for a while, she had trouble controlling her emotions and couldn't concentrate. Now when she is having trouble concentrating and is emotional, she can comfort herself and tell herself that the distressful experiences won't last forever.

for you to do

Healing from your current trauma may be easier if you can remember healing from a past trauma and what helped you.

What past traumas have you healed from? (For example, when you were a kid, you may have been in a car accident that doesn't bother you anymore.)

_____

_____

_____

_____

What are some things that helped you heal from those traumas that might help you heal from this trauma (for example, talking to your parents, spending time with friends, getting enough sleep)?

_____

_____

_____

_____

_____

_____

_____

Sometimes it can seem that intentionally doing the work to heal from a trauma is too much trouble. This exercise is to help you weigh the advantages and disadvantages of healing from trauma at this time. Complete each of the columns by writing as many ideas as you can think of.

Advantages of working to heal from this trauma now	Disadvantages of working to heal from this trauma now	Advantages of not working to heal from this trauma now	Disadvantages of not working to heal from this trauma now
Example: *I will be able to concentrate on my schoolwork this semester.*	Example: *I may get upset, and people will want to know what's wrong.*	Example: *I can try to avoid thinking about it and can focus on other stuff.*	Example: *I may have to deal with it later, when it's even more inconvenient.*

You probably wrote something in each of the columns, but now you can use all of the information you wrote down to figure out the best plan for you. Don't just choose the column that has the most ideas, but look at all that you have written and make the choice that's best for you. If you still aren't sure you are ready to heal from this trauma, it's okay to continue to work through some of the skills in this book. Then you can make your decision before the processing of the trauma starts.

My plan at this time is to:

_____ *Move ahead and process the trauma to heal completely as soon as possible.* If this is your choice, move ahead to the next activity.

_____ *Move ahead through the skills and then decide about processing the trauma when the time comes.* If this is your choice, move ahead to the next activity.

_____ *Wait to do anything. I'm not ready right now.* If this is your choice, that's okay. This book will be here when you need it.

4 reacting to trauma: fight, flee, and freeze

for you to know

People react to frightening, dangerous, and traumatic situations differently than they react to other situations. Reactions to traumatic situations are always in three categories: fight, flee, or freeze. These responses happen automatically and are controlled by a primitive part of your brain. You don't get to choose which response you use.

Jacob is hurt in a car accident. When the paramedics arrive to help him, he tries to fight them and keep them away from him for the first few minutes after the crash. He later understands that they are there to help him, and he allows them to take him to the hospital. Once he gets to the hospital, he can't make sense of why he would fight with people who were trying to help him.

When she smells smoke and hears the fire alarm in her house, Samantha is so frightened that she runs out of the house and down the street. She doesn't even notice that she is running until she gets to the end of her street. She waits until after the fire department arrives before she moves closer to the house to find the rest of her family.

Nick was sexually abused by his soccer coach. When the coach first touched him inappropriately, Nick froze and was unable to move or talk. Now he feels bad for not fighting to keep the coach away from him and for not firmly saying, "No!" Since he didn't fight or say no, Nick is afraid to talk about what happened to him. He worries that people will think that he wanted the inappropriate touching to happen.

for you to do

How would you explain to Jacob that his reaction is normal and expected?

_____

_____

_____

_____

How would you explain to Samantha that her reaction makes sense even if she didn't realize at the time what she was doing?

_____

_____

_____

_____

What would you say to Nick to explain that you understand that he didn't want the touching to happen?

_____

_____

_____

_____

...and more to do

What reactions did you have when you were in frightening, dangerous, or traumatic situations? Describe your reactions on the following lines and write the type of reaction (fight, flee, or freeze) before each reaction.

_____ Reaction:

_____

_____

_____

_____

_____ Reaction:

_____

_____

_____

_____

If you had additional reactions, you can note them here:

_____

_____

_____

_____

_____

Can you now explain any of your reactions as fight, flee, or freeze reactions that you didn't understand when they were happening? If so, you can describe them here:

_____

_____

_____

_____

_____

_____

_____

_____

5 remembering trauma

for you to know

One of the reasons we react so strongly to trauma is that our brains are set up to store memories about trauma differently from memories about nontraumatic events. Trauma memories are stored as sense memories. You may remember sights, sounds, tastes, touches, smells, body sensations, or body positioning.

Although any sense can trigger a trauma memory or a strong reaction, smells are often especially tied to trauma memories. It's common for you to remember the smells that you smelled during the trauma. It would also be common for a similar smell to remind you of the trauma and make you think about it or react to it again.

The memories don't always have words with them, or you may find them difficult to describe in words. Also, these memories may not come in order from beginning to end.

Memories of trauma are often difficult to start and stop on purpose. You may find yourself thinking about the trauma without meaning to, and you might have trouble stopping the memory when you want to.

The purpose of working through the rest of this book is to process your traumatic memories and change them so that they are stored more like nontraumatic memories.

Amanda was in a store when it was robbed. During the robbery, a jar of pickles got broken, and now every time Amanda smells something like pickles, she gets very scared and has flashbacks of the robbery.

Drew is bullied at school and is often physically assaulted by some boys there. When he finally reports the assaults to the assistant principal, it's hard for Drew to remember what happened during each assault, and he feels as if he were viewing disconnected pictures of the assaults instead of a video.

for you to do

Think about a memory that was not traumatic, maybe your last birthday party.
What do you notice about the memory? Do you remember events in order? Do you
remember conversations or physical feelings more? Are there specific sense memories
from that situation or not? Are you able to shift your thoughts to something else if you
want to?

_____

_____

_____

_____

_____

_____

_____

_____

_____

_____

_____

If you are comfortable doing so, think about what happens when you remember the trauma you experienced. What do you notice about that memory? Do you remember events in order? Do you remember conversations or physical feelings more? Are there specific sense memories from that situation or not? Are you able to shift your thoughts to something else if you want to? Is how you currently remember the traumatic event different from how you remembered it right after it happened?

_____

_____

_____

_____

_____

_____

What other differences do you notice between traumatic and nontraumatic memories?

_____

_____

_____

_____

_____

thinking and remembering

for you to know

After you've experienced a trauma, it's common to keep thinking about what happened over and over again. Remembering like this can happen in different ways and is expected after a trauma.

Often the memories happen when you are awake, and they may distract you from what you are doing or from what people are saying to you. Sometimes the memories come when you are asleep, in the form of nightmares. Sometimes the memories are so strong that it feels as if you were back in the traumatic situation and the trauma were happening all over again. This scary kind of memory is sometimes called a *flashback*. Sometimes these memories cause reactions in your body, like tight muscles and a fast heartbeat, or intense feelings, like fear, anger, or sadness. Remembering the trauma may be distressing, but you will start to think about the trauma less and less over time and as you learn new skills to help you manage.

Brittany notices that she is having trouble concentrating at school ever since she was assaulted by her boyfriend. She finds herself thinking about her boyfriend and the assault. She's not doing well in her classes, and even little jobs around her house, like making her bed, are taking more time than usual. She is trying to keep in mind that this reaction is normal and will slowly go away now that the trauma has ended.

Dan has trouble breathing normally and feels really scared and angry when he drives past the park where he was jumped and robbed of his MP3 player. He passes the park every day and is really getting tired of his reactions.

Lizzie has been having nightmares since she witnessed a car accident that killed a classmate. She keeps waking up several times a night after having a nightmare in which she hears and sees the crash again. It takes her a long time to go back to sleep, and she sometimes doesn't even want to go back to sleep because she knows the nightmare will come back. She has learned to use skills to manage the nightmares and to get back to sleep faster when she does have them.

for you to do

Put check marks next to the ways that you have remembered your trauma, both right after the trauma and right now.

I did this right after the trauma.	I'm doing this now.	
		I think about the trauma all the time.
		I think about the trauma when I am trying to think about other things.
		I'm having trouble concentrating on other things because I'm thinking about the trauma.
		I'm having nightmares about the trauma.
		I'm having other scary dreams, even if they don't seem to be about the trauma I experienced.
		I'm having flashbacks about what happened, in which I feel as if the trauma were happening again.
		I have physical reactions (like sweating, fast breathing, fast heartbeat, muscle tension, and so on) when I remember the trauma.
		I have intense feelings (sadness, anger, fear, and so on) when I remember the trauma.
		Other ways I've been reexperiencing the trauma:

...and more to do

When have you noticed that you were thinking about or remembering the traumatic event that happened to you? Example: *I think about it more when other people ask about it or when my level of overall stress is worse.*

_____

_____

_____

_____

_____

What makes your memories, flashbacks, or nightmares worse? Example: *Not getting enough sleep and spending too much time alone.*

_____

_____

_____

What makes your memories, flashbacks, or nightmares better? Example: *Spending time talking to my friends, going to therapy, getting exercise.*

_____

_____

_____

_____

What ideas do you have that you think will help you manage your memories, flashbacks, or nightmares? Example: *Taking a warm bath before going to bed.*

_____

_____

_____

_____

_____

_____

_____

for you to know

Often, thoughts and memories after a trauma are uncomfortable and upsetting, so people frequently try not to think about the trauma. There are many ways you might try to avoid thinking about or remembering the trauma.

Here are some of the ways you might avoid thinking about and remembering the trauma:

- You avoid conversations about the trauma and the people who might want to have those conversations with you.

- You sleep as much as possible to keep from thinking about the trauma.

- You even turn to alcohol or drugs to try to help yourself to avoid thinking about or feeling the trauma.

- You avoid people, places, or activities that remind you of the trauma.

- One extreme way to avoid thinking about or remembering the trauma is to be unable to remember important parts of the traumatic event. You may not be able to explain exactly what happened or the order the events happened in. The memories might come back, but they might not.

- You might stop being interested in or having fun doing activities that you used to enjoy.

- You might find yourself able to have only a limited number of feelings. For example, you may not be able to feel happy, and may only feel scared, sad, and angry.

- Finally, you may stop being able to see your future and may even start thinking that you won't have a normal future like everyone else.

Joey was assaulted on the way home from school. Ever since it happened, he has been having stomachaches in the mornings, so he stays home from school. He also avoids walking down the street where the assault occurred. When he has to go to school, he smokes marijuana after his last class, before walking home, so that he can relax and not have to think.

Taylor was sexually abused by her mom's boyfriend when she was in elementary school. She never talks to anyone about what happened. She has been asked several times if she was ever abused, but she continues to deny that she was abused because she can't think about it or talk about it with anyone.

for you to do

Put check marks next to the ways that you have avoided thinking about or remembering your trauma, both right after the trauma and right now.

I did this right after the trauma.	I'm doing this now.	
		I try not to think about the trauma.
		I try not to feel any feelings about what happened.
		I try not to talk with anyone about what happened.
		I try not to do any of the activities that I was doing when my trauma happened.
		I try to stay away from the place where the trauma happened.
		I try to stay away from other places that I associate with the trauma (like the place where I was when I talked about the trauma for the first time).
		I try to stay away from people that were there when the trauma happened.
		I try to stay away from people who I know will want to talk to me about the trauma.
		I try to stay away from people who remind me about the trauma in some other way.
		I can't remember all of what happened to me when I was traumatized.
		I'm not interested in activities that I used to enjoy.
		I'm not interested in activities that I used to think were important.
		I don't feel connected to or attached to my family anymore.
		I don't feel connected to or attached to my friends anymore.
		I can't feel happy, excited, or other positive feelings anymore.
		I don't think I'm going to have a normal future like other people.
		I don't think I'm going to live as long as other people.
		I'm using alcohol or drugs to keep from thinking about or feeling the trauma I experienced.
		Other ways I have been avoiding memories of the trauma:

...and more to do

What have you noticed about what you have been avoiding? Example: *I haven't talked to the person who used to be my best friend, because she was the first person I told about what happened and I don't want to talk about it anymore.*

_____

_____

_____

_____

Sometimes avoiding is okay, but sometimes you need to do things even when you don't want to. What are some things that you know you need to do even when you don't want to? Example: *I don't want to talk about what happened, but I have to testify in court and tell the truth.*

_____

_____

_____

_____

Who are some people in your life you can count on to help you get out and stop avoiding when you need to? Example: *Parents, friends, therapist, a couple of teachers.*

_____

_____

_____

_____

being jumpy and on edge

for you to know

After the trauma you experienced, you might have found yourself being more jumpy and on edge than usual. This can make it hard for you to sleep, cause you to jump at loud noises, and make you grouchy or irritable. You may also start seeing more danger in the world than you did before the trauma, and then spend time watching out for that danger.

Tyler witnessed a shooting. Now he notices that he jumps and becomes very anxious when he hears loud noises that remind him of the sound of a gunshot. He also notices that he always looks around him, even during class. Because of these reactions, he's falling behind in school since he can't keep his mind on his work.

Megan was sexually assaulted while on a date at a school dance. Ever since this event, she notices that she is having difficulty sleeping. Sometimes the sleep problems are because of nightmares, but other times she just can't fall asleep. Megan's parents notice that she yells at them and at her siblings, and also gets angry with her friends. As time goes on, Megan slowly becomes less irritable and angry, but she's still having trouble at school because she is very afraid of people coming up behind her. She tells one of her friends about her fear, and her friend agrees to stand behind Megan while she is at her locker. Megan is then able to get her things from her locker without fear, and she starts to feel better at school too.

for you to do

Put check marks next to the ways that you have been jumpy and on edge, both right after the trauma and now.

I did this right after the trauma.	I'm doing this now.	
		I have trouble falling asleep.
		I have trouble staying asleep.
		I am irritable and easily annoyed.
		I get angry more easily than I used to.
		I have trouble focusing or concentrating on the things that need my attention, like schoolwork.
		I feel that I need to watch for danger around me all the time.
		I jump at loud noises.
		Other arousal symptoms:

...and more to do

What helps you calm down when you are feeling jumpy and on edge? Example: *Going to a yoga class, calling my best friend.*

_____

_____

_____

_____

Do you have any ideas about what might help you with your arousal symptoms, such as how Megan asked her friend to watch her back when she was at her locker?

_____

_____

_____

_____

Are there people who can help you when you are having arousal symptoms?

_____

_____

_____

_____

9 do you have PTSD?

for you to know

You may have heard of PTSD and wondered what it was and if it applied to you. *PTSD* stands for *post-traumatic stress disorder* and is one of many mental health diagnoses that can be applied as a result of being exposed to trauma. To be diagnosed with PTSD or any of the other conditions that occur from being exposed to trauma, you must see a medical doctor or mental health professional, like a counselor, therapist, psychologist, or social worker.

PTSD is a collection of the reactions and symptoms we talked about in previous activities, like avoiding reminders of the trauma, having intrusive thoughts and nightmares, and being jumpy and on edge. For your reactions to qualify as PTSD, they must significantly interfere with your normal functioning for a time. PTSD is often used on television and other media sources to explain all reactions to trauma, when that's not always an accurate description. Depression, for example, is another mental health diagnosis that's common after exposure to trauma.

An important thing for you to remember about PTSD and any other diagnosis that you receive as a result of being exposed to a trauma is that these diagnoses are usually not permanent. While some mental health disorders are *chronic*, meaning that they can be treated but never go away completely, PTSD and other reactions to trauma usually go away completely. The difference is similar to having a physical injury, like a sprained ankle, compared to having a physical disability, like cerebral palsy. Both conditions may make it necessary for you to use crutches, but the sprained ankle will heal, while the disability is usually chronic.

Hannah was in her house when it was hit by a hurricane. She got out of her house okay physically, but is having a lot of thoughts and nightmares about the hurricane and feels irritable, jumpy, and angry all the time. She starts going to a therapy group at her school for students with PTSD. She asks the group leader, a school social worker, about PTSD. Hannah feels better knowing that so many people have had similar reactions to traumatic events that the reactions have a name (PTSD).

for you to do

Make a check mark next to all of the problems you are currently having because of the trauma you experienced.

	Having thoughts or memories of the trauma pop into your head even when you don't want them to
	Having nightmares about the trauma
	Experiencing flashbacks
	Having physical reactions (fast breathing, fast heartbeat, tight muscles) when you are reminded of the trauma
	Experiencing intense feelings (sad, mad, scared) when you are reminded of the trauma
	Avoiding thoughts, feelings, or conversations about the trauma
	Avoiding anything (people, places, activities) that remind you of the trauma
	Being unable to remember important parts of what happened
	Being uninterested in activities you used to enjoy
	Feeling detached from other people
	Being unable to think about a future for yourself
	Having difficulty sleeping
	Being irritable or angry (more than before the trauma)
	Having difficulty concentrating
	Being jumpy and on edge

If you checked off more than six of the previous reactions, you may want to talk with a medical doctor or mental health professional to see if you have PTSD and to get some help with your symptoms.

...and more to do

Is it important to you to know if you could be diagnosed with a mental health condition? Why or why not?

_____

_____

_____

_____

_____

Some people are relieved to learn that the problems they are experiencing have a name, while others think that having a diagnosis means something bad about them. What would it mean to you if you found out that you had PTSD or some other diagnosis?

_____

_____

_____

_____

_____

building support systems 10

for you to know

One of the most important things that you will need in order to heal from your trauma is a support system. In fact, how good a person's support system is often predicts how quickly and how well he will heal from a trauma. Your support system can be made up of your family, your friends, and even people you haven't met yet. Developing and using your support system is going to be an important part of your healing.

Brandon was sexually abused by his uncle. His family is supportive of him, but he doesn't like talking to them about his thoughts and feelings. He often thinks that he must be strange or weird, because he doesn't know any other boys who have been sexually abused and he used to think it happened only to girls. Brandon even sometimes misses his uncle and the special gifts and activities he offered to keep him from talking about the abuse.

Brandon eventually starts going to a therapist who runs a group for other boys who were sexually abused. Although Brandon doesn't know the other boys well or have a lot in common with them, it's nice for him to have a place where he can go once a week to talk about the sexual abuse with people who really understand what he has been through. By going to the group, Brandon learns that his reactions are common and that most of the rest of the people in the group have experienced similar reactions.

Kayla is walking to school when she and two of her friends are hit by a car driven by a drunk driver. Kayla and the other two girls weren't very close friends before, but become very close as a result of the incident. They start spending a lot of time together and help support each other through difficult times. Even a long time after the crash, when they stop spending as much time together, they are able to depend on one another when they need to, even in the middle of the night. Getting support from her friends and being able to support them help Kayla heal from the crash.

for you to do

Who is currently a part of your support system?

Family Members	Friends	Other People

Pick six of the people in your support system, two from each of the categories above, if possible, and write what they do that feels supportive to you.

Support person 1: _____

What this person does:

_____

_____

_____

_____

Support person 2: _____

What this person does:

_____

_____

_____

_____

Support person 3: _____

What this person does:

_____

_____

_____

_____

Support person 4: _____

What this person does:

_____

_____

_____

_____

Support person 5: _____

What this person does:

_____

_____

_____

_____

Support person 6: _____

What this person does:

_____

_____

_____

_____

What if you notice that you don't have very many people as part of your support system? This is not uncommon, but it's very important that you start to build a support system for yourself. Whom would you like to become a part of your support system? What would each of those people do for you?

_____

_____

_____

_____

What can you do to add that person or those people to your support system?

_____

_____

_____

_____

_____

_____

11 talking about trauma

for you to know

Sometimes people don't tell other people—even those very close to them, like their parents—about the traumas they have experienced. Usually the only way to get help is to tell someone what happened to you.

People have different reasons for not talking about trauma. The most common reasons are:

- They're embarrassed that the trauma happened or about discussing their reactions.

- They were doing something they were not supposed to be doing when the trauma happened.

- They feel as if they have no one to tell.

- They're worried about the reactions of the people they might tell.

- They have been threatened not to tell or are afraid of the consequences of telling.

David was at a party with some people he didn't know that well when his parents thought he was spending the night at a friend's house. There was a fight at the party, and a girl got shot. David can't seem to get the memory of the shooting out of his head and is having trouble at school. He doesn't want to tell his parents about what he saw, because he worries that he will get into trouble for being at the party. He eventually tells his parents and they are upset that he lied to them, but they are supportive of him and sorry that he saw something so terrible.

Lauren is sexually abused by her older cousin when their families are together at a reunion. Her cousin warns her that if she tells anyone about the sexual abuse, no one will believe her. He adds that because he has a scholarship to college, getting in any trouble will ruin his life.

Lauren needs some help dealing with the abuse, but is hesitant to tell anyone. She doesn't want to talk about the sexual abuse because it's embarrassing, she doesn't want to ruin college for her cousin, and she's worried that her parents and the extended family won't believe her. Lauren really wants to talk to someone about what happened. She eventually talks with a school counselor, who tells the police and Lauren's parents what happened. At first, Lauren's mom doesn't believe her, but Lauren gets the support she needs from other people until her mom is able to believe her.

for you to do

If you have already told someone:

What were the reactions of the people you told? Were their reactions helpful or unhelpful?

_____

_____

_____

_____

_____

Is there anyone else you want to tell? Who? How will you tell that person?

_____

_____

_____

_____

_____

If you haven't told anyone yet, use this table to think through the pros and cons of telling someone.

Pros of telling	Cons of telling	Pros of not telling	Cons of not telling
Example: *I won't have to see the person who hurt me anymore.*	Example: *I might have to talk to the police.*	Example: *I won't stress out my family members.*	Example: *I won't be able to get the professional help I need.*

Whom are you thinking of telling? How will you tell that person? What do you hope the reaction will be? What if the person's reaction is different?

_____

_____

_____

_____

12 asking for help

for you to know

Most people need some help while they are healing from trauma. The steps to asking for help are (1) deciding what kind of help you need, (2) choosing the person who can help you, and (3) asking that person for the specific thing you need her to do. Sometimes healing from trauma is easier if you have help from a professional. These professionals have many titles, like counselor, therapist, psychologist, social worker, or psychiatrist.

A classmate rapes Stephanie when they are at a party over the summer. When she gets her schedule for the fall, Stephanie finds out that he will be in one of her classes. She decides that she needs to change classes and is aware that the school principal already knows about the rape. She asks the principal to move her to a different class, and the principal makes the change through the school counselor so that Stephanie won't have to tell the school counselor directly what happened.

James was in a car accident and, ever since then, is having a lot of trouble concentrating in school. He's also arguing with his parents and fighting with people at school. He is having trouble sleeping because memories about the accident come only when he is trying to sleep. His parents talk to him about going to a therapist. At first James doesn't want to go because he thinks people who talk to therapists are "crazy," but he agrees to go at least a few times.

James talks with Ryan, a social worker, who helps him understand that his experiences are common reactions to trauma. James and Ryan meet every week for an hour. Ryan gives James some exercises to try and other things to do to help him manage his reactions. After a few months, James feels much better and his life has returned to "normal," so he stops meeting with Ryan.

for you to do

What do you need help with?

_____

_____

_____

Whom can you ask to help you?

_____

_____

_____

How are you going to ask that person for help? Be sure to be specific about what you need the person to do.

_____

_____

_____

What are your beliefs about therapy and the people who go to therapy? Are there any reasons you would not go to therapy? Are you sure that your reasons are based on facts and not opinion?

_____

_____

_____

_____

How will you know if you need extra support from a counselor or therapist later, even if you don't think you need it now?

_____

_____

_____

_____

How will you let your parents know if you decide that you need extra support?

_____

_____

_____

_____

…and more to do

What are some qualities that you would like your therapist or counselor to have?

_____

_____

_____

What are some questions you can ask potential therapists to figure out whether they have the qualities you listed?

_____

_____

_____

_____

_____

_____

13 healthy and unhealthy coping skills

for you to know

After trauma, we use healthy and sometimes unhealthy activities and behaviors to cope. The coping skills we use can help us understand what we need. We can then choose healthy coping methods if we need to replace some unhealthy ways of coping.

Ever since she was traumatized, Rachel doesn't want to be around anyone and just wants to forget what happened. She isolates herself and spends all the time she can in her room, even telling her parents that she is sick so that she doesn't have to go to school. Rachel realizes that drinking alcohol helps her to sleep and to keep from thinking about her trauma. She starts drinking every day to keep from thinking about it.

With some help from her best friend, Jenn, Rachel realizes that she is isolating herself because she doesn't feel safe around most people and that she has been drinking to keep from thinking about the trauma. Jenn agrees to stay with Rachel at school to help her feel more comfortable. Rachel agrees to squeeze Jenn's arm when she is thinking about the trauma, and Jenn agrees to respond by talking with Rachel about something unrelated to the trauma, especially funny things, to keep Rachel from thinking about it too much. This plan allows Rachel to stop isolating herself and to stop drinking alcohol.

for you to do

List the coping skills you are currently using, how they help you, and whether they are healthy or not. If they are not healthy, try to think of healthy coping skills you might use instead. You'll find an example in Rachel's story.

Coping skills	Purpose	Healthy? Yes or no	If no, a healthy replacement
Isolating myself, staying in my room.	Makes me feel safe.	No, it's causing my grades to drop, and I miss my friends.	Going back to school but making sure that a friend is always with me.

Are there any new coping behaviors that you want to add?

Healthy coping skill	Purpose
Going to kickboxing class	*Makes me feel strong and able to defend myself; good exercise*

…and more to do

Taking your current behaviors and turning them into coping mechanisms is a great way to feel better. For example, if you imagine the stress from your trauma washing off of you every time you take a shower, you will lower your stress level by doing something (showering) that you were probably going to do anyway.

What are some things you already do that might work as coping mechanisms to help you heal from your trauma?

_____

_____

_____

_____

_____

_____

_____

_____

_____

14 crisis plans

for you to know

During the process of healing from your trauma, there may be times when you are in crisis and need help. It's best to plan for those situations ahead of time so that you know what to do.

Justin sometimes has intense reactions when he remembers his traumas. The memories sometimes make him have panic attacks, cry, or hyperventilate. He makes arrangements with all of his teachers so that he can leave the classroom and go to the school social worker's office by just handing them a note card that he carries with him. His teachers all agree not to stop him or make him talk, but he is just allowed to leave when he needs to. Justin is worried at first about asking his teachers because he doesn't want to have to tell them what happened to him, but they all agree to his plan and he only tells them that a trauma happened to him.

Nikki was sexually abused by her father for many years. After she told someone what was happening, he was arrested, but since then he was bailed out and is living at a friend's house until the trial. Even though he isn't supposed to go near her, Nikki is worried that she might see her father.

She sets up a crisis plan with her closest friends. If any of them sees her father or if Nikki just starts feeling uncomfortable when they are out somewhere, they will leave immediately. Her friends also agree that Nikki won't have to go anywhere alone, including to the bathroom, and they stay with her to make sure that she is safe. They also make sure that one of them always has a phone handy with which to call the police if necessary.

for you to do

Create crisis plans for these situations and any others that you think you might need.

At school:

_____

_____

_____

At home:

_____

_____

_____

At work:

_____

_____

_____

Out with friends:

_____

_____

_____

At practice, meetings, or other activities:

_____

_____

_____

Other:

_____

_____

_____

Other:

_____

_____

_____

for you to know

When you experience or remember trauma, your body releases chemicals that trigger the fight, flee, or freeze reaction. Controlled, deep breathing helps signal your brain and body that you are safe, and ends the fight, flee, or freeze reaction. There are many ways to practice controlled, deep breathing.

noticing your breath and taking deep breaths

The first and most important breathing skill is to just notice your breath. Notice how your breath is when you are relaxed. Are your inhalations and exhalations the same length, or is one longer than the other? What parts of your body move when you breathe? What else do you notice about your breath? If you can, notice how your breath is when you are thinking about the trauma? How is your breath different from when you are relaxed?

Next, start to take controlled, deep breaths on purpose. If possible, it's easiest to practice this while lying down on your back in a place where you are comfortable. Put one or both of your hands on your stomach, and imagine that there's a balloon in your stomach. Slowly breathe in so that your chest, lungs, and the balloon in your stomach fill up. Slowly breathe out so that the balloon, your lungs, and your chest completely empty out. You might want to imagine that you are blowing out a lot of birthday candles in order to slow down and control your exhalations. Continue breathing in this way for at least ten breaths. Once you are comfortable breathing this way while lying down, you can practice it when you are sitting and standing.

for you to do

Practice the breathing skill you just learned several times a day for a few days, and answer the following questions:

What did you like about this skill?

_____

_____

_____

What didn't you like about this skill?

_____

_____

_____

For what nontrauma-related situations might you use this skill (for example, *Before a test* or *Before asking my parents for something I want*)?

_____

_____

_____

For what trauma-related situations might you use this skill (for example, *When I think I see the person who hurt me, When I wake up from a nightmare*)?

_____

_____

_____

...and more to do

Here are some variations on the breathing skills. You might decide to practice each one to see what works the best for you in different situations.

chest/tummy breathing

After you have practiced taking deep breaths, you can easily check your breathing by putting one hand on your chest and one hand on your stomach, and noticing how they are moving when you breathe. If you are taking shallow breaths, just your chest will be moving. You can work to slow and deepen your breathing until both of your hands are moving. Often, after practicing this skill for a while, just putting your hands on your chest and stomach will signal you to slow and deepen your breathing.

breathing and counting

Another way to make sure that your inhalations and exhalations are the same, and to slow your breathing, is to count while you breathe. Count slowly while you inhale. There's no correct number to start with, but you will probably count to between three and six as you inhale. Then count slowly as you exhale. Work to control your breathing so that you inhale and exhale the same count. After you have practiced this, you can practice slowing your breathing by increasing the count for each inhalation and exhalation. You can also see what happens if you exhale for one more count than you inhale. Some people find this even more calming, but others do not, so you can see what you experience.

16 calming skills

for you to know

Calming and grounding your body can help you manage your reactions to a trauma. Calming and grounding skills bring your attention to the present rather than to what happened in the past. There are many ways of calming and grounding your body.

5-4-3-2-1

Name five things you can see in the room. Name them in some detail, if possible. Name five things you can hear right now. Name four things you can see. Name four things you can hear. Name three things you can see. Name three things you can hear. Name two things you can see. Name two things you can hear. Name one thing you can see. Name one thing you can hear.

Or try the following optional variation.

room search

Pick a color and then name all of the items in the room that you can see that are that color. The variations to this practice are endless. You can choose a picture and name all of the colors that you see in it. You can name all of the things that you see that start with a particular letter. You can count the number of objects in the room as you name them all. The idea is just to bring your whole, focused attention to your present location and to let go of the distractions of other places and times.

for you to do

Practice one of these skills a few times a day for a few days, and answer the following questions:

What did you like about this skill?

_____

_____

_____

What didn't you like about this skill?

_____

_____

_____

For what situations might you use this skill?

_____

_____

_____

There may be times when you want to use your skills in ways in which no one else can notice. You may be in a situation where you don't want to bring attention to yourself or don't want other people to notice that you are upset, but you need to use your skills to calm yourself. For the 5-4-3-2-1 skill, think about how you could do it in a way that no one else might notice, and answer these questions:

How could you do this skill so that no one else would notice (for example, *I could write the things I see and hear on a piece of paper during school*)?

_____

_____

_____

For what situations might this skill be helpful (for example, *When I feel anxious during school because of some memories but think I can stay in class if I can just calm down*)?

_____

_____

…and more to do

Here are some additional ways for you to calm and ground yourself when you are upset.

focusing on grounding

Sit in a comfortable chair, with your feet flat on the floor. Notice how you are connected to the ground. Feel your feet on the floor. Feel the back of your legs against the bottom of the chair. Feel your back against the back of the chair. Feel your arms on the arms of the chair. Notice how the chair supports and connects you to the ground. Breathe. Continue to focus on the way you are connected to the ground. When other thoughts come in, gently bring your thoughts back to how you are connected to the ground. Continue to breathe and notice how you are connected to the ground until you are feeling calmer.

body scan

Scan your entire body slowly in your mind. Describe the sensations that you feel in each part of your body. Don't try to change the sensations, but notice whether they change on their own. Try not to judge whether the sensations you are feeling are good or bad; just notice what you are feeling. But heed this caution: this can be a difficult skill for people who have been sexually abused.

Practice one of these skills a few times a day for a few days, and answer the following questions:

What did you like about this skill?

_____

_____

_____

What didn't you like about this skill?

_____

_____

_____

For what situations might you use this skill?

_____

_____

_____

_____

How could you use this skill without anyone else noticing?

_____

_____

_____

for you to know

Trauma and related memories can cause tension to be stored in your muscles. It's important to learn to relax your muscles to help yourself heal from the trauma. There are many ways of relaxing your muscles.

progressive muscle relaxation

Get into a comfortable position, either sitting or lying down. Start at your head. Take a few deep breaths. Tighten the muscles in your face. Hold them tightly for a few seconds and then relax them. Take a few deep breaths. Tighten the muscles in your neck and shoulders. Hold them for a few seconds and then relax them. Take a few deep breaths. Tighten the muscles in your hands and arms. Hold them for a few seconds and then relax them. Take a few deep breaths. Tighten the muscles in your torso (chest, back, and stomach). Hold them for a few seconds and relax. Take a few deep breaths. Tighten the muscles in your upper legs. Hold them for a few seconds and relax. Take a few deep breaths. Tighten the muscles in your lower legs and feet. Hold them for a few seconds and relax. Take a few deep breaths. Scan your body for any other places of tension. Tighten each of those places, hold for a few seconds, and then relax. Take a few more deep breaths. When you are ready, move around in a way that feels comfortable and continue your day.

tightening and relaxing all your muscles

Tighten all of your muscles at one time. Hold them for a few seconds and then relax. Repeat this tightening and relaxing three to five times until your whole body feels relaxed.

tightening and relaxing specific muscles

Many people have tension in specific areas of their bodies. If you notice that you have a specific area of tension, you can tighten and relax just that area of tension. Tighten the muscles, hold them for a few seconds, and then relax.

for you to do

Practice each of these skills a few times a day for a few days each, and answer the following questions.

Progressive muscle relaxation:

What did you like about this skill?

_____

_____

_____

What didn't you like about this skill?

_____

_____

_____

For what situations might you use this skill (for example, *After going to bed to help me go to sleep*)?

_____

_____

_____

_____

Tightening and relaxing all your muscles:

What did you like about this skill?

_____

_____

_____

What didn't you like about this skill?

_____

_____

_____

For what situations might you use this skill (for example, _Before getting out of my car after getting to school_)?

_____

_____

_____

_____

Tightening and relaxing specific muscles:

What did you like about this skill?

_____

_____

_____

What didn't you like about this skill?

_____

_____

_____

For what situations might you use this skill (for example, *Before starting on a math quiz that I am nervous about*)?

_____

_____

_____

...and more to do

There may be times when you want to use your skills without anyone else noticing. For these relaxation skills, think about how you could do them without anyone else noticing, and answer these questions:

How could you do this so that no one else will notice?

_____

_____

_____

For what other situations might these skills be helpful?

_____

_____

18 soothing skills

for you to know

Trauma makes our minds and bodies tense and anxious. It's important to have activities that you like to do that help soothe this tension and anxiety. Doing things that you enjoy with each of your five senses can help manage your tension and anxiety most effectively.

for you to do

The following activities engage each of your five senses. Circle the ones that you already do and enjoy. These are things that may help you control any tension and anxiety you have. Write a check mark next to activities that you think you might want to try but aren't currently doing to manage your tension and anxiety. In the blank lines, add activities that you already do or that you would like to try.

Vision Activities

☐ Watching a sunset

☐ Reading a favorite book

☐ Watching a funny movie

☐ Looking at a favorite picture

☐ Watching television

☐ Reading a magazine

☐ _____

☐ _____

Hearing Activities

☐ Listening to music

☐ Listening to waves

☐ Listening to kids playing

☐ _____

☐ _____

Touch Activities

☐ Petting a dog or cat

☐ Taking a warm bath

☐ Sitting in the sun

☐ Wearing a favorite shirt

☐ Squeezing a stress ball

☐ Exercising

☐ _____

☐ _____

Taste Activities

☐ Drinking calming tea

☐ Chewing spearmint gum

☐ Eating chocolate

☐ Eating a favorite food

☐ Brushing your teeth

☐ Eating a ripe piece of fruit

☐ _____

☐ _____

Smell Activities

☐ Smelling a flower

☐ Lighting a scented candle

☐ Smelling freshly cut grass

☐ _____

☐ _____

...and more to do

Activities that engage more than one of your senses are even better. Try to think
of some things you could do that might engage more than one of your senses, for
example, going for a run while listening to angry music, and noticing what you see
and smell on the route.

_____

_____

_____

_____

_____

_____

taking good care of your body 19

for you to know

After trauma, it's important to take good care of your body. This will help your brain and body heal. You need to get enough sleep, eat healthy food, get fresh air and sunshine, and use moderation (don't go to extremes) in these efforts.

Ever since she was traumatized, Lexi has felt really depressed. She wants to sleep all the time, doesn't exercise, eats only junk food, and avoids going outside at all. With the help of her family and friends, she starts to go for walks outside in the afternoon and begins eating healthier food. She also makes an effort to stay in bed no more than ten hours a day. Slowly, these efforts help Lexi feel healthier and more in control, which helps her heal from her trauma.

Ever since his trauma, Will has felt very vulnerable. He thinks (incorrectly) that if he had been stronger, he wouldn't have been a victim. Will starts working out all the time, spending hours each day at the gym. He ignores his homework and other responsibilities so he can work out. He pretends to go to sleep, but then gets up and works out in his room at night. He changes his diet to help himself gain muscle, but stops eating any of the food he used to like. Because he overtrains, Will gets injured and ends up feeling more vulnerable. When his injury heals, he starts training again but uses more moderation and is able to feel stronger and more in control, which helps him heal from his trauma.

for you to do

Look at each of your own current habits to see if you need to make changes to take better care of your body.

Getting the right amount of sleep: Teens need between eight and ten hours of sleep per night.

☐ *I get too much sleep.*

☐ *I get about the right amount of sleep.*

☐ *I get too little sleep.*

What I am going to do to change my sleep habits:

_____

_____

Eating healthy food: Teens should eat at least three meals per day that include a variety of foods. Most of the food should be healthy, but it's important to also eat foods that you enjoy.

☐ *I need to add more healthy food.*

☐ *I get about the right amount of healthy food.*

☐ *I need to add more foods that I enjoy.*

☐ *I get about the right amount of foods I like.*

What I am going to do to change my eating habits:

_____

_____

Getting fresh air and sunshine: It's important to get some time outside every day, if possible, and to get a moderate amount of sunshine during the week.

☐ *I need to get more fresh air and sunshine.*

☐ *I get about the right amount of fresh air and sunshine.*

What I am going to do to change these habits:

_____

_____

Moderation: It's important that you do all of your habits in moderation.

What I am going to do to add some moderation to my habits:

_____

_____

...and more to do

What things are you doing to take good care of your body that you can combine with other skills, like deep breathing and muscle relaxation, to help you heal from trauma? Example: *I have to walk to school, so I'll walk quickly and breathe deeply to get some exercise and fresh air, and to practice deep breathing to help me heal.*

_____

_____

_____

_____

_____

_____

_____

_____

_____

_____

_____

activating helpful parts 20
of your brain

for you to know

One part of your brain, the *amygdala*, is responsible for your reactions to trauma and memories of trauma. Another part of your brain, the *frontal lobe*, is responsible for thinking and planning. Scientists have learned that these two parts of your brain cannot be active at the same time. You can learn to start controlling your reactions to trauma and related memories by intentionally activating your frontal lobe.

Ever since he was sexually abused, Nathan gets overwhelmed with anger and fear whenever he thinks about the abuse. He also thinks about the abuse a lot more than he wants to. Nathan learns that doing math problems helps him calm down. At times he writes down hard problems to do, but sometimes just adding up the numbers of the license plate on the car in front of him while he is driving is enough to distract him and to activate his frontal lobe in order to stop his reaction to the trauma.

Torrie was bullied and assaulted at school, so she has a hard time concentrating when she remembers how she was treated. Torrie learns that making lists of things helps her to not think about the trauma so that she can think about school. Torrie makes lists of colors, animals, things that start with the letter "T," even lists of things she can make lists of. These lists help Torrie calm down and be able to concentrate in school.

for you to do

Think of at least five ways that you can calm yourself and concentrate, as Will and Torrie did:

_____

_____

_____

_____

_____

When you notice yourself starting to react to the trauma you experienced or related memories, try one of the ways to calm yourself that you listed in the last step, and then answer these questions:

What did you try?

_____

Was this helpful to you?   Yes   Partly   No

If it was helpful, in what other situations will you use it?

_____

_____

_____

If it was partly helpful or not helpful, what will you try the next time you find yourself starting to react to trauma?

_____

_____

_____

What did you try?

_____

Was this helpful to you?   Yes   Partly   No

If it was helpful, in what other situations will you use it?

_____

_____

_____

If it was partly helpful or not helpful, what will you try the next time you find yourself starting to react to trauma?

_____

_____

_____

What did you try?

_____

Was this helpful to you?   Yes   Partly   No

If it was helpful, in what other situations will you use it?

_____

_____

_____

If it was partly helpful or not helpful, what will you try the next time you find yourself starting to react to trauma?

_____

_____

_____

...and more to do

Take a few minutes to observe the world around you in detail. This is another skill that can help you calm down. Notice what you can see, hear, feel, smell, and maybe even taste. Notice the variations in colors that you see, the temperature of the air, and as many details as you can.

After your observation, notice how you are feeling, what changes you saw in yourself, and how calm you are.

_____

_____

_____

_____

_____

_____

_____

21 finding a safe space

Ever since her trauma, Amber doesn't feel safe leaving her house. She does remember a quiet ocean beach where she used to go with her family, and she recalls having felt totally safe and calm there. She practices thinking about being at this beach. She remembers how the sand felt under her feet and how the sun felt on her shoulders. She recalls the sounds of the waves, the wind, and the birds. She thinks about the smell of the ocean. She remembers how everything looked, especially how the water shimmered and sparkled in the sun. Whenever she thinks about this beach, she feels safe and calm, which enables her to leave her house to do the things she needs to do.

Tony has never actually felt safe in his life. Having experienced a lot of trauma in a lot of situations, he doesn't have any memories of a place where he felt safe. He makes up a room where he can feel safe, and he practices imagining himself there. The room doesn't always make sense—for example, it doesn't have any doors or windows—but this is what Tony needs the room to be like to help him feel safe, so it's good that way. Tony makes sure he knows how the room looks, smells, sounds, and feels to make the visualization as vivid and real as possible. Tony is then able to think about his room when he needs to feel safer and calmer in order to go about his day. It's important that Tony think about his safe room only in situations where he is pretty safe, like school, not in situations where he really is in danger.

for you to do

Think about what your safe place is or what it might be like. Answer these questions about it. Be as vivid and detailed as possible.

Where is your safe place?

_____

_____

What does it look like?

_____

_____

_____

What does it smell like?

_____

_____

_____

What does it sound like?

_____

_____

_____

What does it feel like?

_____

_____

_____

_____

Practice thinking about your safe place when you are feeling unsafe or uncomfortable, or are having thoughts or memories about the trauma—but only when you are really safe. Notice how doing this helps you feel calm, safe, and relaxed.

...and more to do

When are you going to practice thinking about your safe place?

_____

_____

_____

Some people need more than one safe place; for example, they need one that's outside and one that's inside. What's another safe place you might think about using for other situations?

_____

_____

_____

_____

_____

_____

_____

22 making good decisions

for you to know
It's important to have a procedure for making good decisions. Especially after experiencing a trauma, it's a good idea to have a decision-making procedure that you can use when it might be difficult for you to think clearly and concentrate well.

The steps to making good decisions:

1. Identify what the question really is. What are you really trying to decide?

2. List all of the possible options. For this step, you don't want to include outrageous options that you know you would never do, but you do want to include all of the options that you are willing to consider.

3. List the pros and cons of each option. Almost all options will have both pros and cons.

4. Choose the best option. Don't just choose the option that has the most pros or the fewest cons from step 3, but really pay attention to what the best option is by looking at all of the pros and cons.

5. Make sure that you have included all of the pros and cons for the option you have chosen, that you have considered what's best both in the short term and the long term, and that this is really the best option. If it isn't, go back to step 4 and pick another option.

6. Do what you have chosen to do.

7. Look back. Was there anything you missed when you decided to do what you chose to do? Is there anything you would want to consider next time you need to make a decision?

for you to do

Use this step-by-step guide the next time you are making a difficult decision. Some examples are included to help you.

Step 1: Identify what the question really is. Example: *Should I go to the party at Robbie's house, even though I know my friends there will be drinking, which might remind me of when I was sexually assaulted last summer at a party when I was drinking?*

_____

_____

_____

_____

Step 2: List all of the possible options. Example: *Go to the party and drink, go to the party and don't drink, find something else to do, or stay home and do nothing.*

_____

_____

_____

_____

_____

_____

_____

Step 3: List the pros and cons of each option. See the examples in the following table, and then come up with similar pros and cons for each of the options you listed in step 2.

Options	Pros	Cons
Go to the party and drink.	*I'll be able to spend time with my friends.* *People will think I'm doing okay.* *I can drink, which will help me feel calmer and less nervous.*	*I get really nervous around crowds and situations that remind me of being sexually assaulted.* *I might lose control if I'm drunk.* *I might be in danger again if I'm drunk.*
Go to the party and don't drink.	*I'll be able to spend time with my friends.* *People will think I'm doing okay.* *I'll be able to stay in control to help me keep safe.*	*I get really nervous around crowds and situations that remind me of being sexually assaulted.* *I might want to drink to help myself calm down.*

Step 4: Choose the best option. Example: *I'll go to the party, but I won't drink.*

_____

_____

Step 5: Make sure. Example: *As I look at the pros and cons again, I can see that this really is the best option for me in both the short and long terms. I realize that since I'll still be nervous, it will be good to have a person I know and trust at the party with me. I'll invite a friend to go with me who knows about the sexual assault and who can help me feel more comfortable.*

_____

_____

_____

_____

Step 6: Do what you have chosen to do.

Step 7: Look back. Example: *After the party, I realized that it would have been easier if I had thought beforehand of reasons I could give for not drinking. It would have also been a good idea to plan with my friend who came with me something I could say that would tell her that I needed to go in another room to take a break or that I needed to leave.*

_____

_____

_____

_____

...and more to do

What are some situations in which you struggle to make decisions? How can the process you just learned help you?

_____

_____

_____

_____

After using this process several times, have you noticed any patterns in what you forget to consider once you look back? What can you learn from that?

_____

_____

_____

_____

_____

_____

Even though thoughts and memories about trauma can pop into your head without warning, it's not always a good time to think about the trauma. It's important for you to be able to temporarily put away the intrusive thoughts and memories that are bound to come up. These container skills will help enable you to put the intrusive thoughts and memories away temporarily until it's a better time to think about them.

Alyssa was sexually abused by her uncle for a few years, and even though it happened a long time ago, she still has thoughts about the abuse when she is trying to focus in school or when she is with her friends and boyfriend.

Alyssa first gets herself a container to put the thoughts and memories into. She chooses a spaghetti sauce jar that her family used a few nights before. She picks the jar because it has an airtight lid, and it's important to her that what she puts in there can't get out. Alyssa also wants something that will fit in her backpack, because she thinks she might take it with her to use at school. She also likes that she can see what's in the jar, since she doesn't like to be surprised by anything anymore. Alyssa starts using her jar by writing down the intrusive thoughts and memories, and putting the paper in the jar. This helps Alyssa to contain the intrusive thoughts and memories as she goes about her day.

As Alyssa gets better and better at this skill, she is able to just think about putting the intrusive thoughts and memories into her jar, rather than actually writing them down and putting them in. Just thinking about something rather than doing it is called visualization. Sometimes the visualizations aren't as effective, and she actually needs to write down the thought and put it in the jar. As she practices the skill more and more, she gets better at it and is able to put away the intrusive thoughts and memories as they happen.

Alyssa also uses her container visualization (imagining thoughts going into her jar) before she goes to bed each night. Putting into her jar any thoughts from the day that are still bothering her and any worries she has about the next day helps her to sleep more soundly.

for you to do

Pick a container, and practice writing your thoughts and memories on paper and then putting the paper into your container.

What is your container? Why did you choose this container? Is there another one that might work better for you?

_____

_____

_____

After you have practiced writing your thoughts and memories on paper and putting the paper into your container, you can start to visualize (imagine) the thoughts and memories going into your container.

What did you notice when you switched from the paper to visualization?

_____

_____

_____

...and more to do

Alyssa used her container skill before going to sleep. What are other situations or events for which it might be good for you to use your container skill?

_____

_____

_____

_____

_____

_____

_____

_____

_____

24 when feelings are overwhelming

for you to know

After you've experienced a trauma, your feelings can be overwhelming. However, feelings are natural, normal, and one of the ways we experience the world. Trying to avoid feeling your feelings often makes the feelings worse.

Nate was sexually abused by a friend's father. Ever since the abuse was discovered, he hasn't been allowed to see his friend. Sometimes he feels sad because of the loss of his friendship. Whenever Nate tries to ignore his sad feelings, he notices that he feels even sadder and overwhelmed by his sadness when he doesn't want to be sad, like when he's hanging out with his new friends.

for you to do

The following is a list of feelings. Look at the list and add feeling words that you sometimes have. Then, circle the five feelings you have the most often.

Happy	Sad	Angry	Scared
Proud	Depressed	Furious	Nervous
Excited	Glum	Frustrated	Terrified
Joyful	Lonely	Jealous	Disconnected

Look at the feelings you circled and write them at the top of each of the following columns. Then describe how you know that you are feeling that feeling. Be sure to include what your body feels like when you are feeling that feeling.

Feeling	How I know I'm having it

...and more to do

Feelings can sometimes seem overwhelming (as if you will never stop crying or stop feeling afraid). This can be especially true if you think about times in the past when you felt the same feelings and times in the future when you might feel the same way. You may think about avoiding your feelings altogether, but they will almost always come back even stronger. What can be helpful is to feel your feelings and acknowledge them without thinking about the past or the future. The best way to do this is to concentrate on what you are feeling in your body and notice how your feeling changes.

The next time you have a strong feeling, just sit and notice what your feeling is and how it feels in your body. If your thoughts shift away from the feelings in your body, don't worry about it, but bring your attention back to your body. Notice what happens to your feelings.

What happened when you were able to sit with your feelings?

_____

_____

_____

_____

_____

Many people guess that their feelings will keep getting stronger and stronger if they don't try to push them away. What happened when you didn't try to push your feelings away and just noticed them?

_____

_____

_____

spotting unhelpful thoughts

for you to know
Thoughts are constantly and automatically going through our heads. We then make assumptions and interpretations of those automatic thoughts, and these assumptions and interpretations influence how we feel and act. Not all of the assumptions and interpretations we make are true, and recognizing errors in our thinking can help us feel better and act the way we want to.

Jonathan sends a text to Sam, and Sam doesn't respond. When Jonathan sees Sam at school the next day, Sam doesn't say anything about the text. Jonathan assumes that Sam doesn't like him and doesn't want to be friends, and that this must be why Sam hasn't texted him back. Jonathan stops hanging around Sam and feels terrible every time he sees him.

Austin sends a text to Dylan, and Dylan doesn't respond. When Austin sees Dylan at school the next day, Dylan doesn't say anything about the text. Austin assumes that Dylan was grounded from his phone and never saw the text. Austin asks Dylan if he got the text and Dylan confirms that he was grounded from his phone, so they are able to talk in person about what was in Austin's text.

Courtney paid attention in driver's ed, always tried to follow the traffic rules, and was a careful driver. Still, she was in an accident, and her friend was badly hurt. Courtney thinks that it isn't worth trying to do anything anymore, because bad things will happen no matter what. As a result of these thoughts, she stops working at school and her job. Her grades fall, and she is fired from her job. Courtney believes even more that bad things will just keep happening in her life and that she has no control over anything.

for you to do

Can you think of a time when you assumed something that influenced your feelings or actions, and later learned that your beliefs were inaccurate or incorrect? What was the situation? What did you learn from that experience?

_____

_____

_____

_____

_____

_____

There are a lot of different types of thinking errors, but here are a few that are very common.

Extreme thinking: This is when you think in extremes, like if you don't get a perfect score, you are a complete failure.

An example of a time I did this was…

_____

_____

_____

_____

Catastrophizing: This is when you believe that one bad thing is going to lead to more bad things until everything is eventually terrible. For example, you might think that because you forgot to turn in a math assignment, you will fail the class, and then you won't graduate and will end up being unable to go to college.

An example of a time I did this was...

_____

_____

_____

_____

Jumping to negative conclusions: This is when you think about only the bad or negative options that are possible, as Jonathan did in the example. The opposite of this example was Austin's scenario, where the same events led to different thoughts and feelings.

An example of a time I jumped to negative conclusions was...

_____

_____

_____

_____

...and more to do

While it's helpful to recognize errors in our assumptions and interpretations, it's also helpful to then be able to come up with a better explanation of the situation. One of the best ways of doing this is to look for the proof that your thought is true. For example, Jonathan might have felt better if he had looked for proof that Sam was upset with him. If he did that, he would have realized that whenever Sam had been upset with him in the past, Sam talked to him directly, so he probably didn't text back for some other reason.

What proof did Courtney have for her belief that it wasn't worth it to put effort into activities?

_____

_____

_____

_____

What proof did Courtney have that it might be worth it to put effort into activities?

_____

_____

_____

_____

Not all thoughts that are connected to negative feelings are connected to errors in beliefs, assumptions, or interpretations. Especially after a trauma, it's important to look at evidence to see whether or not your thoughts contain thinking errors. For example, it wouldn't be a thinking error for Courtney to believe that some things were out of her control, but it is a thinking error for her to believe that all things are out of her control and that her efforts have no effect on anything. Her thinking error is being extreme in her belief that *none* of her efforts have an effect. Sometimes it takes someone outside the situation to point out the possible thinking errors.

Think about a situation around which you have strong feelings. What thoughts, assumptions, beliefs, and interpretations do you have about that situation?

_____

_____

_____

_____

_____

_____

_____

Whom could you talk with about your thoughts, assumptions, beliefs, and interpretations to make sure they are accurate?

_____

_____

_____

26 how thoughts, feelings, and actions are connected

for you to know

Thoughts, feelings, and actions are connected, and each can change the other. The following diagram shows how they are connected.

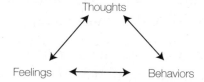

Most people pick up books like this because they want to change how they feel. Feelings are difficult to change directly, but changing what we are thinking or doing can change how we feel.

Alex feels anxious about going back to school after being bullied and beaten up. He decides to change his thoughts in order to change his feelings, so he reminds himself that the bullies were expelled and his friends have a plan to make sure he isn't alone between classes. Alex feels better knowing this, and his anxiety decreases.

Becca feels depressed and sad after being paralyzed in a car accident. She spends time chatting with her friends on the computer when she is depressed, and this helps change her mood.

for you to do

Write down a situation in which you commonly have strong feelings that you want to change. This situation can be related to the trauma you experienced or not. Example: *My friends stop talking when I walk up to them.*

_____

_____

_____

Write down the thoughts that automatically pop into your head, and also the assumptions and interpretations you make about those thoughts. Example: *They must be talking about me. They must not like me. There must be something wrong with me.*

_____

_____

_____

Write down a different interpretation of what happened. Example: *Maybe they had just finished whatever they were talking about, and it just happened to be at the same time that I walked up.*

_____

_____

_____

How might that change your feelings?

_____

_____

_____

Now, instead of changing what you are thinking, come up with ideas about how you can change what you are doing that might change your feelings. Example: *I could go talk with another friend.*

_____

_____

_____

...and more to do

It may seem simple to change what you are thinking or doing in order to change your feelings, but sometimes it's difficult, so it's good to plan ahead.

What if you are sure that your thoughts, assumptions, and interpretations are correct? What could you do to change your feelings? Example: *I could check with someone whom I trust and who supports me to see if that person agrees with my thoughts, assumptions, and interpretations.*

_____

_____

_____

_____

What if you are in a situation, like sitting in class, where it might be difficult to do something different in order to change your feelings? What can you do (or think) that will help change your feelings?

_____

_____

_____

_____

27 thought records

Kelsey was in a car that was hit by a drunk driver. She thinks she is healing well from the accident, but notices herself reacting in a really negative way whenever people ask her how she is doing. She uses the following thought record to help her understand her reactions.

Steps to Completing a Thought Record:

1. Identify the situation around which you have a strong negative feeling. Who was involved? Where were you? What was happening?

2. Write down the feelings you are having. Don't forget that you will probably have more than one feeling and the feelings might even seem contradictory.

3. Rate the feelings on a scale from 1 to 10, where 1 means just a little of the feeling and 10 means the most you could ever imagine feeling the feeling.

4. Write down the thoughts you are having. Don't stop yet to see if the thoughts make sense; just write down the thoughts that come into your head about the situation.

5. Circle or underline the thought that seems to have the most to do with your change in feelings.

6. Check to make sure that this thought is accurate. In most cases, it won't be accurate. You can look for evidence that it is true. If it really is an accurate thought, go back to your list of thoughts and pick one that is not accurate that's tied to the feelings you are having.

7. Write a more accurate version of the thought you picked in the previous step.

8. Take a little time to think about the more accurate version of your thought. Really try to believe it.

9. Rerate your feelings as you did in step 3. Did they change?

10. Summarize what you learned from this situation.

for you to do

Here is an example of a thought record that has been completed. After the sample thought record is a blank form for you to copy and use on your own. The next time you have a strong shift in your feelings, try using a thought record.

Situation: *Kyle asked me how I was doing today, and I snapped at him.*			
Feelings:	*Mad*	*Annoyed*	*Nervous*
Ratings:	*5*	*7*	*4*
Thoughts: *Why wouldn't I be fine?*			
Everyone knows what happened to me.			
I look like I'm having a hard time after what happened to me.			
What does he want?			
More accurate thought: *Nothing Kyle said really meant that I look like I'm having a hard time. Maybe he was just being nice. Other people said that I looked good and happy, so maybe what happened doesn't show on the outside. People ask each other how they are all the time, and it doesn't mean anything.*			
Feelings:	*Mad*	*Annoyed*	*Nervous*
Ratings:	*1*	*1*	*2*
What you learned: *Even though what happened to me is on my mind a lot, it doesn't always show, and it's not always what other people are thinking about when they talk to me.*			

Situation:			
Feelings:			
Ratings:			

Thoughts:

More accurate thought:

Feelings:			
Ratings:			

What you learned:

...and more to do

Sometimes it might be difficult to come up with more accurate, reasonable thoughts on your own. In those cases, it's often good to get help from trusted and supportive friends or relatives. You might ask them directly what they think might be a more accurate and reasonable thought. You may also just try to think what they might tell you might be a more accurate and reasonable thought.

Who are the people you could ask (or imagine asking) for help with thinking of more accurate and reasonable thoughts?

_____

_____

_____

_____

accomplishing things and having fun 28

for you to know

Changing your behaviors can change your thoughts and feelings. To improve how you are feeling and thinking, it's best to do an activity that you enjoy or an activity that accomplishes something. Activities that involve emphasizing other emotions or intense physical sensations can also be helpful.

When Dani is sad or scared, going out to spend time with friends—something she usually enjoys—is a good activity for her, even if she doesn't feel like going in that moment.

When Kevin is frustrated, he feels better if he cleans his room or gets a little homework finished.

Thomas likes movies. When he is feeling sad or angry, he picks movies that emphasize a different feeling. He doesn't have to just watch happy movies. He finds that watching scary movies is sometimes just as helpful with changing his feelings.

Jasmine used to cut herself to get an intense physical sensation to help herself feel better, but now she knows that riding the roller coaster at the amusement park or putting her elbow in a bucket of ice water can make her feel better without causing damage to her body.

for you to do

List activities that you enjoy doing:

_____

_____

_____

_____

_____

_____

List activities that accomplish something:

_____

_____

_____

_____

_____

_____

...and more to do

Sometimes, as in the examples with Thomas and Jasmine, doing an activity that emphasizes other feelings or an activity that has intense physical sensations can help change your feelings so that you feel a little better.

Pick three feelings and then pick some activities that emphasize those feelings. This will enable you to have a list of activities to pick from that accentuate a different feeling from the one you are having:

_____

_____

_____

_____

_____

_____

List activities with intense physical sensations that do not damage your body:

_____

_____

_____

_____

_____

_____

29 stop avoiding

for you to know

It's common to want to avoid anything that reminds you of the trauma that you experienced. That may involve avoiding people and places that were associated with the trauma, or even people who might ask you how you are doing. For you to fully heal from your trauma, it's important to stop avoiding. Gradually exposing yourself to the people, places, and situations you have been avoiding will help you to fully heal.

Morgan was sexually assaulted in a park. She wants to stop avoiding the park, so she gets her best friend to help her. First they just drive past the park while using skills like deep breathing to help Morgan stay calm and relaxed. Then they sit in the car outside of the park. Then, after Morgan is able to stay calm while sitting in the car, they practice standing outside the car while using skills to help her stay calm and relaxed. Next, they practice walking quickly around the park and leaving, and, later, walking more slowly and staying longer and longer. Anytime Morgan gets frightened or overwhelmed, her friend helps her leave the park, and later they go back to the previous step and practice some more before moving on again. Finally, step by step Morgan is able to spend time in the park with her friends while feeling calm and relaxed.

for you to do

Identify anything that you are still avoiding related to your trauma. This can be a person, a place, a situation, or even a thought or a memory. Now list a step-by-step approach to stop avoiding. When you start going through the steps, take your time, and if you get frightened or overwhelmed, go back a step and repeat that step a few more times before moving forward again.

What are you avoiding?

_____

_____

Step-by-step ways you can gradually stop avoiding:

_____

_____

_____

_____

_____

_____

_____

What are you avoiding?

_____

_____

Step-by-step ways you can gradually stop avoiding:

_____

_____

_____

_____

_____

_____

_____

_____

What are you avoiding?

_____

_____

Step-by-step ways you can gradually stop avoiding:

_____

_____

_____

_____

_____

_____

_____

_____

...and more to do

As you move through the steps toward the things you have been avoiding, it's important that you stay calm and relaxed. The following questions may help you stay calm and relaxed. You may have different answers for each thing you identified that you are avoiding.

What does your body feel like when you are calm?

_____

_____

What does your body feel like when you are anxious, worried, frightened, or overwhelmed?

_____

_____

What skills help you stay calm (for example, *deep breathing, listening to music*)?

_____

_____

_____

What people help you stay calm?

_____

_____

_____

_____

for you to know

Talking about, thinking about, and writing about the trauma on purpose makes it become much less overwhelming, because you get used to the thoughts and feelings that come up and you know what to do about them. Calming your reactions when you think about the trauma will eventually connect the trauma to feeling calm instead of feeling frightened, sad, overwhelmed, or whatever feelings you have when you think about your trauma.

Since working her way through this book, Brianna has gained skills and knowledge that have prepared her to begin to actively work though her trauma by writing and rewriting her story. She is still worried about thinking of the trauma on purpose, especially since she spends so much time trying not to think about what happened to her. Brianna makes lists of skills and activities that help her feel calm so that she can calm herself down if she starts to get upset whenever she thinks about the trauma while processing it.

for you to do

Here are some things to consider when you are deciding whether you are ready to begin processing your trauma by thinking, talking, and writing about it on purpose.

Do you have a good support system? Example: Do you have people you can talk to about your thoughts and feelings who understand you and can distract you in helpful ways? Is there anyone else you need to add to your support system?

_____

_____

Do you want to work through this story on your own, or do you want some help to do this? A big part of working through the story of the trauma is being able to recognize and change assumptions and beliefs that might not be true. If you struggle with this, it might be good to have some help. If you want some help, whom can you talk to in order to get that?

_____

_____

Do you have helpful habits for coping with your feelings and memories? Are these habits healthy? Are your unhealthy coping habits under control?

_____

_____

Are you taking good care of your physical body? Do you need to add or take away anything to take better care of yourself?

_____

_____

Look at the following list of skills and activities, and rate how you feel about your ability to accomplish that skill when needed:

Skill or activity	I'm confident in my ability to use this skill or do this activity effectively.	I know this skill or how to do this activity, but I might need some more practice.	I don't know how to use this skill or do this activity.
Breathing skills			
Calming skills			
Relaxation skills			
Soothing skills			
Activating the helpful (frontal lobe) part of your brain			
Safe-space visualization			
Process for making good decisions			
Container for trauma			
"Sitting with" your feelings			
Noticing your thoughts			
Challenging your inaccurate thoughts			
Changing your feelings by changing what you are thinking or doing			
Completing thought records			
Doing activities you enjoy			
Doing activities that accomplish something			
Doing activities that emphasize other feelings			
Doing activities that have intense physical sensations			

Other things you know to do or to think about that help you feel calm even when you are thinking about the trauma:

_____

_____

_____

_____

_____

_____

Based on your answers to the previous questions, you can decide for yourself whether you are ready to begin to work through your trauma by thinking about it, talking about it, and writing about it on purpose. You don't necessarily have to have mastered every skill on the list, but you will want to make sure that you feel ready. If there are skills you would like to review or add, all of the skills just listed are in the earlier chapters of this book, and you can go back and review them.

...and more to do

It's common to want to avoid working through the trauma, especially since working through it involves thinking and talking about the trauma on purpose. If you have the skills you need but are still avoiding, make a list of small steps you can take toward working through your trauma, and then start to do them one at a time while managing your emotions, just like the examples in the previous chapter.

for you to know

It's important for you to be able to tell your whole story about the trauma you experienced. Many people decide to write their stories on paper or use a computer. These ways are great, but there are other ways too. You may decide that painting, drawing, writing poetry, making a film, or even dancing is the way you want to tell your story. The instructions included here will be for writing the story on paper, but you can choose the way that makes sense to you.

Because he has his own computer, Kyle decides to write his story using his computer. He also likes to draw, so he decides that he might draw some parts of the story of his trauma to go with his written words.

Kate likes to write in her journal and finds it soothing to write things out by hand. She knows that when she handwrites, her thoughts slow down, which feels better to her. She decides to write out her story by hand.

for you to do

Now is the time for you to tell your story. Write out your story in as much detail as you want. You will add parts to it later. It may take you many sessions to get your whole story on paper.

Remember, it's important for you to be calm and relaxed as you write, so if the memories start to upset you, if you start to feel afraid, or if you just think you need a break, stop and come back to it another time.

When you have finished a session of writing, be sure to put the story away both literally and symbolically. You may want to use a container skill from activity 23 or some of the other skills you know to specifically end the time you spend thinking about the trauma and start thinking about something else.

...and more to do

Now that you are working on creating the written version of your story, you may have noticed that you need to use more skills to manage your reactions. Next, make a check mark to indicate skills that you have tried that were helpful, skills that you have tried that weren't helpful, and skills that you might want to try soon.

Skill or activity	I tried this activity, and it helped me.	I tried this activity, and it didn't help me.	I might want to try this activity to see if it helps.
Breathing skills			
Calming skills			
Relaxation skills			
Soothing skills			
Activating the helpful (frontal lobe) part of your brain			
Safe-space visualization			
Process for making good decisions			
Container for trauma			
"Sitting with" your feelings			
Noticing your thoughts			
Challenging your inaccurate thoughts			
Changing your feelings by changing what you are thinking or doing			
Completing thought records			
Doing activities you enjoy			
Doing activities that accomplish something			
Doing activities that emphasize other feelings			
Doing activities that have intense physical sensations			

32 adding to your story

for you to know

For the telling of your story to be the most effective in helping you heal from your trauma, it's important that it contain a lot of specific details. Adding details about what you sensed, thought, and felt during the traumatic event will ensure that you work through the trauma as much as possible so that it doesn't bother you in the future.

Alexandra experienced a trauma that happened only one time, so she is able to add what she sensed, thought, and felt during the event, and doesn't have to skip over any parts.

Jordan experienced a trauma that happened many times over several years. He uses the second list (which you'll see shortly) to make sure that he adds what he needs to but doesn't have to write out every single event that occurred.

for you to do

Go back and add details to your story. After each sentence that you have already written, see if there is more that you can add. You can add details in any order you want, but make sure that all details are added before moving on. This may take you quite a while to get all of the details included. Check off each item on the list as you finish it.

For everyone:

- What did you see then? (Then move on a sentence or two, and ask the question again.)

- What did you hear then?

- What did you smell then?

- What did you taste then?

- What did you touch then?

- What did your body feel like then?

- What were you thinking then?

- What were you feeling then?

For people with more than one related traumatic incident, make sure to include:

- The first time

- The last time

- The time you remember the most vividly

- The worst time

- At least one time for each location where it happened

- Any time that something significantly different happened

Remember, it's important for you to be calm and relaxed while you are writing, so if the memories start to upset you, if you start to feel afraid, or if you just think you need a break, stop and come back to it another time.

When you have finished a session of writing, be sure to put the story away both literally and symbolically. You may want to use a container skill from activity 23 or some of the other skills you know to end the time you spend thinking about the trauma and start thinking about something else.

...and more to do

Remember that you can choose whom to show your story to. It's very important that you add significant details to your story, even if they are things you never want another person to see. Avoiding these details now may be troubling to you in the future. Go back through your story and add any details you might have avoided. You may have to add these details in small steps, the way you have managed other things you were avoiding, and that's okay.

for you to know

It's very common to have thinking errors in trauma stories. The thinking errors are part of what makes the trauma so difficult for people to endure. By finding and challenging these thinking errors, you will progress in your healing from your trauma. Some common thinking errors are:

There was something I could have done to stop or prevent what happened.

I am responsible for what happened.

I am damaged because of what happened to me.

Everyone can tell that something happened to me.

for you to do

Every situation is different, but the thinking errors from traumatic events are pretty common. Look at the examples of common thinking errors and read through your story to see if you thought any of these things or something similar. You might want to underline or highlight them.

Now look at those thoughts again to see if you still think them. If you don't still believe those things, add a sentence about what you currently think. For example, if you thought at the time of the trauma that it was your fault, you could write, "Now I realize that I was a child and he was an adult, and I didn't have control in the situation, so it couldn't be my fault."

If you had thoughts that seem similar to the thoughts in the examples but are not sure whether they are thinking errors, you might need to do some investigation. There are several ways of doing this:

- Look for evidence that your thought was true. Look for evidence that it was false. What conclusions can you reach?

- Ask a trusted person what she thinks.

- Pretend that your best friend was telling you about the situation that you experienced. If he told you that he was thinking the thought that you had, would you agree that it was an accurate thought, or would you challenge him that it was a thinking error?

Now see if you can come up with more-accurate thoughts for the thinking errors you have identified.

...and more to do

If it's comfortable for you to do so, have a trusted person read through your story, and ask her to look for thinking errors you might have missed. If this isn't possible, set your story aside for a few days, and then reread it to try to notice thinking errors you might have missed.

---

for you to know

We are changed by the traumatic events that we have experienced and by healing from them. Some, but not all, of those changes are bad. Sometimes real learning and growth come from very hard situations.

Eric was sexually abused by someone he thought really cared about him and was his friend. Now he has trouble trusting adults who want to get close to him.

Madison was mugged on the subway on her way to school. After that happened, she took some self-defense classes and practiced standing up for herself. She is now much more confident, even if she can't guarantee that she won't get mugged again.

for you to do

Check off each of the following changes that you see in yourself as a result of the trauma:

☐ *Difficulty trusting people*

☐ *Avoiding people who are reminders*

☐ *Interested in new things*

☐ *Not interested in things I used to care about*

☐ *Isolating*

☐ *Avoiding places that are reminders*

☐ *More confident*

☐ *More aware of my surroundings*

☐ *Less confident*

☐ *Closer to my family and friends*

☐ *Met new people*

☐ *Know who my true friends are*

List some of the other changes that have happened to you as a result of your trauma:

_____

_____

_____

_____

...and more to do

If there are any changes you noticed in the previous list that you don't want to keep in your life, identify them and make a plan for changing them. For example, if you have difficulty trusting people you don't know, you may decide to try to talk to one person you don't know every week so that you can learn to trust your own judgment again.

Changes you don't want to keep and your action plan:

_____

_____

_____

_____

_____

_____

35 staying safe

---

for you to know

It's important to have good skills to say no to bad situations in order to keep yourself as safe as possible. This doesn't mean that the trauma that happened to you was your fault or could have been prevented, but it's good to have the best skills and plans possible for future situations.

Juan wants to make friends and fit in, just as most teens do. He also knows that he doesn't want to use drugs and alcohol. He comes up with ways to say no to his friends that include speaking firmly, looking them in the eye, and saying what he means. He also practices saying exactly what he will say if he is offered drugs or alcohol: "No, thanks, I don't use or drink." In case he finds himself in a situation he needs to get out of, he and his parents also come up with a plan where he can call them and they will come get him, no questions asked.

for you to do

Identify situations in which you might need to say no or keep yourself safe. For each situation, list what you would say, how you would say it, and how you would get out of the situation.

Situation:

_____

What you will say:

_____

_____

How you will say it:

_____

_____

How you will get out of the situation:

_____

_____

_____

Situation:

_____

What you will say:

_____

_____

How you will say it:

_____

_____

_____

How you will get out of the situation:

_____

_____

_____

Situation:

_____

What you will say:

_____

_____

How you will say it:

_____

_____

_____

How you will get out of the situation:

_____

_____

_____

36 when you might need more support again

for you to know
Even if you do all of the activities in this book and all reminders of the trauma you experienced are gone, that doesn't mean that you will never be bothered by the trauma again. It's common for trauma to resurface from time to time, and you may need support from friends, family, a therapist, or other people at that time.

Melissa was the victim of a carjacking when she was first learning how to drive. She worked hard and healed from the trauma. The carjacking wasn't bothering her anymore. Then, one of Melissa's friends experienced a carjacking, which makes Melissa start having nightmares again. She is jumpy, feels nervous, and remembers her own carjacking just as she did right after it originally happened. Melissa looks over the skills she previously used that were helpful to her. She also goes back to the therapist she saw in the past, for just a few sessions. In a short time, Melissa is back to normal and isn't bothered by either her own or her friend's carjacking. She just needed some extra support after what happened to her friend.

Aaron was assaulted on a school trip to the state capitol. Years later, when he is an adult, he is scheduled to go on a business trip to the same city. He is feeling anxious and irritable, even though he often travels for business. Aaron talks with a trusted friend, who helps him figure out what his anxiety is about, and then Aaron is able to remind himself that he will be safe and that he is now an adult. This allows him to go on his business trip without any distractions.

for you to do

Try to think about situations that might remind you of your trauma and cause some of the reactions you experienced to come back. Then, identify a plan for what you will do and whom you can ask to help support you.

Situation that might remind you of your trauma:

_____

_____

Whom you can ask for help:

_____

_____

What you will do:

_____

_____

_____

_____

Situation that might remind you of your trauma:

_____

_____

Whom you can ask for help:

_____

_____

What you will do:

_____

_____

_____

_____

for you to know

Sometimes an important lesson or meaning comes from trauma. If you are able to identify some meaning from the trauma that you experienced, it will help you heal more completely and protect you from the negative results of future bad events in your life. Meaning is not something you can always find right away, but it's important to look for it.

Kelsey was sexually abused by her soccer coach. She was very frightened about having told someone, and many people were very angry with her for causing so many problems for someone they liked (the coach). Kelsey stood her ground, and eventually the coach had to go to court and was found guilty of a crime.

One day, Kelsey sees some young girls playing soccer and laughing. She knows that because of what she did, her former coach won't be able to hurt those girls. Kelsey knows that she can't protect everyone, but she is glad that she was able to act to protect people from the person who abused her.

Sam's younger sister was diagnosed with cancer, and after battling the illness for about a year, she died. Sam knows that sometimes his sister had been bored when she was in the hospital. Sam starts raising money to buy video games for kids who are in the hospital. By helping other kids who have the same difficulties as his sister did, Sam is able to find some meaning in the tragedy of losing her.

for you to do

Think about what meaning the trauma you experienced has for you. If you can't think of something right away, that's okay. For your trauma to have meaning doesn't mean that it was good that it happened to you, just that you are making the best of a bad situation.

Ideas you have about the meaning of your trauma:

_____

_____

_____

_____

_____

_____

_____

_____

...and more to do

If you had difficulty finding meaning in your trauma, that's okay. The following questions may guide you to find some meaning, but it's also okay if they don't. Sometimes it takes a while before the meaning of a trauma becomes clear.

What have you learned about yourself from the experience of your trauma?

_____

_____

_____

_____

What have you learned about other people from the experience of your trauma?

_____

_____

_____

_____

Is anyone better off because of what happened to you?

_____

_____

_____

_____

Are you better off in any way because of what happened to you?

_____

_____

_____

_____

Is there some way you are helping other people because of what happened to you?

_____

_____

_____

_____

Is there some way you want to help other people because of what happened to you?

_____

_____

_____

_____

for you to know

You are different from how you were before the trauma happened to you. In many ways, you are also the same as you were before the trauma happened to you. Most people change a lot during their teens, whether or not they experience a trauma. When you are finishing healing from a trauma is a good time to take a look at who you really are.

for you to do

Write the date and answer the following questions. From time to time, you may want to repeat this exercise to see how things have changed.

Date:

_____

Five words that best describe you:

_____

_____

_____

_____

The people who are most important to you:

_____

_____

_____

_____

The way you like to spend your time:

_____

_____

_____

_____

Things you really dislike:

_____

_____

_____

_____

Your strengths:

_____

_____

_____

_____

_____

Your weaknesses:

_____

_____

_____

_____

_____

Where you want to be in one year:

_____

_____

_____

_____

_____

activity 38 ✳ your real self

Where you want to be in five years:

_____

_____

_____

_____

Where you want to be in ten years:

_____

_____

_____

_____

...and more to do

Many people have parts of themselves they are hesitant to let show. What are the parts of you that you are hesitant to let show:

_____

_____

_____

_____

If these parts of you are positive, how can you start to show them to others?

_____

_____

_____

_____

If these parts of you are things you aren't proud of, how can you make them positive and start to show them to others? For example, if you are really opinionated, can you write letters to the editor of your school paper or join the debate team so you can express opinions in ways that aren't likely to offend people?

_____

_____

_____

_____

39 finish your own story

for you to know

The trauma that you experienced is only a small part of who you are and of the experiences that you will have as a person. It was an important part of your life, at least for a while, but there is much more to your life.

for you to do

Finish your story. You can take the story that you wrote about the trauma you experienced, or you can just write about healing from the trauma and the future. You can decide to finish your story using something other than writing, like art or music. Whatever you decide is the best way for you is fine.

...and more to do

Share your story. Decide whom you want to share your story with and do so. It's important for you to share your healing with people, in the same way that it was important for you to share your trauma with them.

Congratulations! You have finished working through this book. The activities will be here if you need to return to them in the future.